# Artlist C

# THE DOG

## NEW YOU FOR THE NEW YEAR

### The Dogs Share Their Health Secrets!

By The Dogs
As told to Sonia Sander

**SCHOLASTIC INC.**

New York    Toronto    London    Auckland    Sydney
Mexico City    New Delhi    Hong Kong    Buenos Aires

ISBN-13: 978-0-545-01183-9
ISBN-10: 0-545-01183-3

10 9 8 7 6 5 4 3 2          07 08 09 10 11

Printed in the U.S.A.
First printing, November 2007

# 🏠 Woof! Woof!

Want to know how we cute and cuddly canines can help you become a brand-new you? Just like you, we have to work at being top dog. We don't become the handsome hounds we are overnight.

We get a little help from our humans, so it's only fair that *we* help *you*. Are you ready?

#  Getting Started

Before we get started, write down your goals. Keep in mind that you can't do it all!

How do we know this? Well, our humans don't try to teach us how to stay, sit, fetch, lie down, and roll over all in the same day. If they did, we would get dog-tired and cranky! Instead, after we master each trick, they reward us and let us rest.

3

# ![paw] A Dog-Eat-Dog World

Like they say, you are what you eat. What you put into your body has a big effect on how you feel! If you eat lots of sugary foods, you may feel a burst of energy — but it won't last.

Humans need to eat foods high in vitamins and minerals. That means more fruits and vegetables, whole grains, and lean meats. It also means avoiding junk foods, which are high in fat and sugars, as much as *paws*-ible.

The same is true for us. Some dog food is higher quality than others. The good ones leave us "lean and mean" and ready to take on the world! Well, maybe just the neighborhood.

# Snack Attack

Snacking is a big no-no. It can *paws*-sibly lead to overeating. Boy, do we know about that! We love food. If you keep refilling our bowl, we won't be able to resist nibbling all day long. Instead of fetching, we'll be huge, lazy, snoozing hounds! *Zzzzzz!*

Your best bet is to curb your eating to set mealtimes. If you are more active on a particular day, you may need a bit of extra fuel. In that case, have a piece of fruit, such as a banana.

## POOCH POINTER

Eating as usual, keep a food diary for a week. Write how each meal made you feel. The next week, cut out junk food and try it again.

Be careful about eating while watching TV. You might be surprised how quickly you'll start to crave food every time you sit in front of the TV.

We dogs know all about that. Once we get a taste for eating scraps from your table, we're hooked. Beware of us begging for a snack. Just one scrap won't be enough! We'll bark and carry on through the whole meal. Eating will become a stressful time for you.

So whatever you do, don't toss us anything from your plate. Our bark is worse than our bite, and listening to us howl during your meal won't be much fun!

# 🏠 Walk the Dog

Feeding your body well is only half the battle. Just like us dogs, you need to get out and exercise. Taking us for a walk means you are helping yourself and us at the same time. Plus it's a great way to make new friends. No one can resist saying hello to cute pooches like us!

We need to walk every day. At your age, you should aim to be active for at least an hour a day. Go on, we double-dog-dare you!

## POOCH POINTER

Make the walk more challenging by walking through sand or shallow water or by walking on, under, or around obstacles.

**11**

# Off the Leash

An hour every day may sound like a lot. But exercise doesn't have to be just walking us. We dogs also get a good workout playing fetch, swimming, or even chewing — but not the furniture or your best pair of shoes.

For you, that means riding your bicycle, playing tag, climbing stairs, cleaning up your room, or playing a sport. Joining a team is another great way to make new friends.

**The best thing you can do is turn off the TV, video games, and computer and get doggone busy!**

# Fit Fur Life

Being fit not only builds your muscles and helps keep you trim, it also helps you sleep better and is a great way to relieve stress.

But remember: Don't get hurt while exercising. Take five minutes to warm up, and then another five minutes to cool down.

Whatever activity you choose, make sure that it's fun for you! If you enjoy it, you'll be less likely to quit.

# Howlin' About Homework

Believe it or not, eating healthy, staying active, and getting a good night's sleep can make doing your homework easier — we *paw*-mise!

If you're feeling dog-tired, you're not going to be focused enough to tackle your homework. You might even doze off and start drooling, like us.

**A+ Dog**

If you start to feel really *grrrr*-umpy or drowsy, take a quick break. Head outside for some fresh air, have a quick nap, or eat a healthy snack.

# Ruff Going

Don't become a procrastinator! As much as we dogs might love to take a walk, play fetch, or learn a new trick, we don't want to stop you from doing your homework.

There's no bones about it! Taking time out to clean your room, watch TV, or call a friend isn't going to make your homework go away or be any easier. In fact, it will do the exact opposite.

The stress of even less time to complete your assignment, not to mention the lost energy you used for the other activity, can make a simple task seem much bigger. So fight the urge to procrastinate!

# Doggy Homework Do's and Don'ts

1. **Do** turn off the TV, radio, and video games and ignore the phone.

2. **Don't** do your homework on your bed, or you'll be snoozing in no time.

3. **Do** set up a special place in your house that's just for homework.

4. **Do** make sure there's enough light in your work space.

5. **Don't** get frustrated if you don't understand something. Instead, ask for help.

# Barking Up the Wrong Tree

We hate to admit it, but we dogs can have a few bad habits! Chewing, for one. When we're puppies, we chew as a part of our teething. It can be hard for us to stop chewing as we get older. We rely on you to help us stop. Telling us "No!" and giving us chew toys helps.

Biting your nails can be a hard habit to break. If you don't notice when you're doing it, you might ask your friends and family to let you know. As soon as they say something, get your hands busy with something else or pop a piece of sugarless gum in your mouth.

**POOCH POINTER**

Keeping your paws — or nails — clean and polished can help you stop biting your nails, too.

#  Friends Fur Life

Making friends can be hard! We're lucky that our humans take care of all of our introductions. Meeting new people all on your own can sometimes seem im-*paws*-sible.

Making new friends takes time, too. The most important thing is to be yourself. Soon you'll have a whole pack of friends to roam and explore the neighborhood with!

## POOCH POINTER

**Here are some great ways to meet new people.**
1. Treat everyone nicely and respectfully.
2. Sit next to someone new on the bus or at lunch.
3. Join a club or sport.
4. Have a party.

# ⌂ Grooming 101

Sometimes it's the little things that can make us feel good about ourselves. Though we dogs may protest when you try to give us a bath or brush our teeth, we feel better afterward. There's just something nice about being sparkling clean from head to toe!

Even if we make a fuss when you wash our beds, we know it's for the best. Just don't try to do it while we're asleep. As the saying goes, let sleeping dogs lie.

# Growlin' Mess

They say you can't teach an old dog new tricks. Some tricks you can't teach us at all! We dogs will never be able to clean up after ourselves. We will always rely on you to fetch our ball or bone from under the couch.

It's different for you and your room. If your room is full of dirty laundry and half-eaten food, you can do something about it.

Don't be so quick to drop your stuff and run. Take the two extra seconds to put the item in its place. If you know exactly where it is, you'll be able to find it lickety-split the next time!

# Reward!

Making changes in your life can be *ruff* going. But when all is said and done, the hard work is worth it!

Plan a reward for each goal you reach. Remind yourself of what it is you're working toward whenever you feel like you might give up.

The rewards can be big or small. We dogs are happy with a pat or a biscuit. You may be happier with a new book, a movie, or a day at the beach. The greatest reward will be when you complete all of your goals.

Feeling better about yourself will make the whole world seem bow-wow brighter and howlin' happier!